RENEWALS 0161 253 7160

RADCLIFFE

Please return/renew this item
by the last date shown.
Books may also be renewed by
phone or the Internet.

www.bury.gov.uk/libraries

explaining...
EPILEPSY

W
FRANKLIN WATTS
LONDON • SYDNEY

LIONEL BENDER

This edition 2013

First published in 2008 by
Franklin Watts
338 Euston Road
London NW1 3BH

Franklin Watts Australia
Level 17/207 Kent Street
Sydney NSW 2000

© 2008 Franklin Watts

ISBN 978 1 4451 1772 0

Dewey classification number: 362.1'96853

Planning and production by Discovery Books Limited
Managing Editor: Laura Durman
Editor: Gianna Williams
Designer: Keith Williams
Picture research: Rachel Tisdale

Printed in China

Franklin Watts is a division of Hachette Children's Books, an Hachette UK Company.
www.hachette.co.uk

Photo acknowledgements: Getty Images: pp. 11 (Nick Veasey), 16 (Pedro Ugarte/AFP), 23 (Stockbyte), 28 (Gary Buss), 36 (Time & Life Pictures); www.HopeForSydney.com: p. 39; istockphoto.com: pp. 14 (Bradley L. Marlow), 19 (Nemanja Glumac), 20 (Dr. Heinz Linke), 25, 27 (Zilli), 31 (Willie B. Thomas), 35 (Gabriel Moisa); www.JohnBirdsall.co.uk: front cover top, front cover bottom left, pp. 9, 13, 18, 30, 33, 34, 37; Science Photo Library: front cover bottom right (Josh Sher), pp. 21 (AJ Photo Hop American), 24 (Mark Thomas)

Source credits: We would like to thank the following for their contribution: Dr. Donald Weaver for Stephen and Colin's stories.

Please note the case studies in this book are either true life stories or based on true life stories.

The pictures in the book feature a mixture of adults and children with and without epilepsy. Some of the photographs feature models, and it should not be implied that they have epilepsy.

Contents

What is epilepsy?

Epilepsy is a condition of the brain. It is caused by a fault in the brain's communication system. The basic symptom of epilepsy is called a seizure. This is a sudden short event where there is a change in a person's awareness, movement or behaviour. During an epileptic seizure, people may be unsure of where they are, what they are doing, their behaviour or their feelings. Sometimes people lose consciousness, fall over and start to shake uncontrollably.

A condition

Epilepsy is a condition. It is not a disease that can be caught from another person. In the United Kingdom, it affects about one in every 103 people. Epilepsy affects people of all ages, but is most common in childhood and in the elderly. During infancy, a child's brain is growing and developing, and it is at this stage that problems can occur that cause epilepsy to develop later. However, epilepsy can also be caused by accidents that involve blows to the head, or by brain tumours.

Definitions

The word 'epilepsy' comes from the Greek word 'epilambanein', meaning to 'seize', or 'take hold of'. A person with a particular type of severe epilepsy can have a seizure that is also known as a fit, a convulsion, an attack or a blackout. The term 'epileptic' is sometimes used to describe a person with epilepsy, but really it should be used only to describe situations arising from the condition, such as an 'epileptic seizure', or in medicines such as 'anti-epileptic' drugs.

The signs of epilepsy

How epilepsy affects people varies. It is often hard for a person with epilepsy to say whether his or her symptoms are mild or severe. Certain kinds of seizures can go undetected, and around half of people with epilepsy do not experience seizures at all.

HIPPOCRATES MAKES THE LINK

A Greek doctor, Hippocrates (460-370 BCE), was the first person to make the link between epilepsy and the brain. Hippocrates is often called 'the father of medicine' because he was the first to understand many of the principles of health and diseases. Today, doctors often sign a modern version of the Hippocratic Oath, a summary of his beliefs, to show their commitment to do the best for their patients.

Epilepsy affects people all over the world. Most people with epilepsy can lead normal lives if their seizures are controlled, and some of them grow out of the condition as they get older.

▲ *People of all ages and races may be affected by epilepsy and there are no outward signs of the condition, apart from seizures.*

Causes and effects

The brain works like a computer: it is probably nature's most complicated machine. It is the body's control centre and is made up of millions of microscopic interconnecting neurones, or nerve cells. Messages pass to, from and within the brain as electrical signals through the neurones. A person with epilepsy can experience a temporary disruption or overload of neurone messages.

The nervous system

Neurones are made of a cell body containing the nucleus, which is the cell's own control centre, and a nerve fibre called the axon. The outer part of the brain, known as 'grey matter', is made up mainly of the cell bodies of the neurones. The inner part of the brain is 'white matter', which is made up of the nerve fibres leading from the neurone cell bodies.

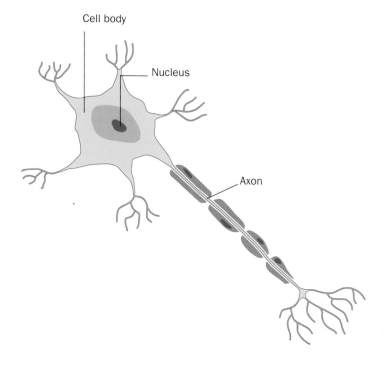

Cell body

Nucleus

Axon

Some of these fibres are short and interconnect with neurones within the brain. Other fibres are more than a metre in length and run down the spinal cord to muscles in the chest, legs and arms. A special group of long fibres, forming the vagus nerve, carries signals to and from the brain, down through the neck, to the digestive system and heart. The brain, spinal cord, nerve fibres and special neurones within muscles and sense organs make up your nervous system.

Synapses

Neurones are packed close together, but do not actually touch each other. There are narrow gaps in between, called synapses. Neurones pass messages to each other across the synapses. Normally, the messages flow in an orderly direction, at regular speed and at a standard strength. In a person with epilepsy, messages become disturbed and disorganised and these changes can cause a seizure.

◄ *A neurone is made up of a cell body and a long nerve fibre called an axon.*

White matter

Grey matter

The distribution of grey matter and white matter in the brain.

Spinal cord

Control centre

Different areas of the brain control different activities in the body. For example, there are areas for speech, memory, muscle action, consciousness and body temperature regulation. Activities such as the beating of your heart, the digestion of food and breathing are all automatic – they happen without any conscious effort. Your senses – including sight, hearing, taste, touch and balance – also work automatically. Other activities, such as walking, switching on a light or playing on a computer, require conscious effort: you think about doing these activities. For a person with epilepsy, the part of the brain affected by seizures can upset one or more of these activity centres and the actions related to them.

Different types of seizures

Epileptic seizures are divided into two main groups: partial and generalised. Partial seizures begin in one area of the brain and sometimes spread to other areas. There are three types of partial seizures: simple, complex and secondarily generalised.

Generalised seizures affect the whole brain and they cause a person to lose consciousness. There are five types of generalised seizures: absence, myoclonic, tonic, tonic-clonic and atonic. Absence seizures used to be called 'petit mal' and tonic-clonic seizures 'grand mal' from the French words meaning 'small illness' and 'great illness'.

Some doctors regard all these terms as too general, because there is a whole spectrum of types of seizures with a wide variety of symptoms.

Causes

Scientists are still not sure exactly what causes problems in the brain's electrical system, or why it happens repeatedly in some people and not in others. About two-thirds of people with epilepsy have no visible physical difference in their brain. One possible cause is an unusual development of the brain or brain damage during a difficult birth. A brain infection or tumour, misuse of drugs, excessive alcohol consumption, or a severe head injury can also cause epilepsy. Older people sometimes develop epilepsy after a stroke.

Who has epilepsy?

Epilepsy sometimes runs in families, which means that it may be an inherited condition. How your body looks and works is determined by your genes.

Genes and DNA

Genes are made up of strands of genetic material called DNA. DNA, which is found inside almost every cell in the body, contains all the information which is passed on from parent to child, such as eye colour, hair colour and nose shape. DNA also contains a code that controls the production of proteins in the body. Proteins are involved in all chemical processes in the body. Sometimes genes do not work properly or get damaged or changed. It may be that epilepsy is caused by these genes.

Inheriting epilepsy

Brothers and sisters, including non-identical twins, share many, but not all, of their genes. It is for this reason that only a small percentage of the siblings of people with epilepsy are likely to experience any kind of seizure in their lifetime. Identical twins have exactly the same genes as each other (see box), so you would expect that if one twin had epilepsy, the other twin would too. This is sometimes, but not always, the case.

In one major study of children with epilepsy, held in Melbourne, Australia, in the late 1990s, scientists found that in 20 per cent of non-identical twins, both children had epilepsy. In identical twins this figure went up to 65 per cent. In the identical twins, the type of epilepsy they both had was almost always the same, making scientists strongly suspect that epilepsy is inherited.

Inheritance of one or more faulty genes can make some people susceptible to epilepsy, but even then, most of these people never experience any symptoms.

GENETIC MAKE-UP

Genes (including those that could cause epilepsy) are passed from one generation to another during sexual reproduction. When an egg from a woman is fertilised by a sperm from a man, the genes of the egg and sperm are combined. Identical twins are the product of one fertilised egg that divides in two, hence the babies that develop have identical genes: the babies are of the same sex, and share the same blood group and same eye colour. Non-identical twins are the product of two separate eggs and two separate sperm. The babies that grow from them have similar, but not identical, genes: the babies may be of different sexes, they may look different and they may have different blood groups.

▲ *Though epilepsy may be inherited, this does not mean that a relative of someone with epilepsy will necessarily have epilepsy too. Even an identical twin of someone with epilepsy may not have the condition.*

Triggers

There seem to be several factors that can set off, or trigger, a seizure, and these are different for each individual. The factors include a lack of sleep or an illness.

High-temperature seizures

Not all seizures are a result of epilepsy. Though one person in 20 has a seizure during his or her lifetime, only one in 50 of those people will be diagnosed with epilepsy. This is because other conditions can

FAMOUS PEOPLE WITH EPILEPSY

The soldiers and statesmen Alexander the Great, Julius Caesar and Napoleon Bonaparte are all believed to have had epilepsy. The Soviet leader Vladimir Lenin had epilepsy. The actor Danny Glover, the comedian Rik Mayall and musicians Martin Kemp and Adam Horovitz also have epilepsy.

also cause seizures. One example of this is febrile convulsions. This happens when children have a very high temperature during an infection. As soon as the child's temperature falls, the seizure ends.

Partial seizures

Partial seizures are seizures that begin in one part of the brain. The person may suddenly become confused or hear odd sounds. He or she may start to tug at their clothes or get up and roam around the room.

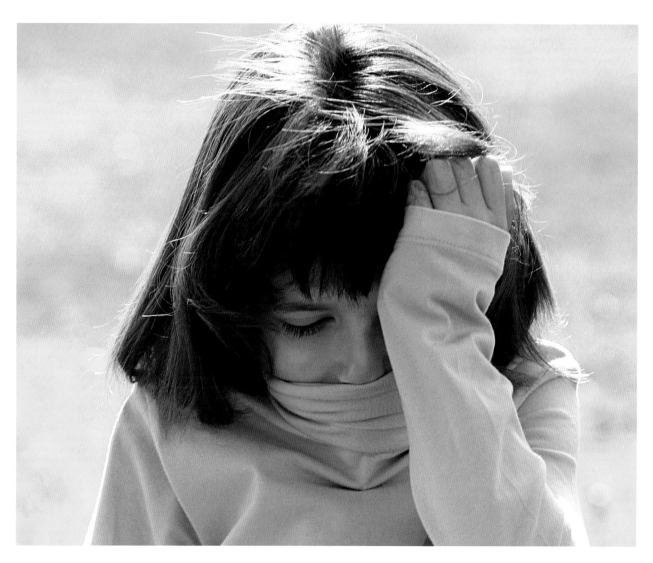

▲ *A child who experiences a partial seizure may feel dizzy for several seconds. The difference between a simple partial seizure and a generalised seizure is that a person does not lose consciousness during a simple partial seizure.*

There are three main types of partial seizure. With many parts of the brain potentially being affected, the symptoms of these seizures are many and varied. Some people have partial seizures with little outward signs so onlookers may not even realise the person is having a seizure.

Simple partial seizures

During a simple partial seizure, a person remains conscious and can remember what happens to them. Simple partial seizures are not necessarily unpleasant experiences. For example, some partial seizures cause only small movements, for example they may cause a person's finger to jerk. During other kinds of partial seizure, a person may smell or taste things that are not there, hear sounds or feel numbness. A simple partial seizure may also cause someone to feel emotions like happiness or fear, for no obvious reason.

Auras

Sometimes a type of simple partial seizure, known as an aura, acts as a warning that the seizure is about to spread to the rest of the brain. Soon afterwards, the person may experience a generalised seizure (see pages 16-17).

Other partial seizures

If the seizure spreads to other parts of the brain, a person can experience two other kinds of partial seizure: complex partial seizures or secondarily generalised seizures.

In a complex partial seizure a person may start to smack their lips, make chewing movements or wander around looking confused. Many people will

tug at their clothing. These seizures can last a few minutes and the person may be tired or confused for a while afterwards.

Secondarily generalised seizures are partial seizures that spread to the rest of the brain and cause a person to lose consciousness and in some cases have convulsions.

Generalised seizures

Generalised seizures are seizures that affect the whole brain from their onset.

They can happen at any time and a person who has one will lose consciousness.

Some people with epilepsy have frequent seizures, others rarely have them.

There are several types of generalised seizures. An atonic seizure is a kind of seizure where a person loses strength in his or her muscles.

A myoclonic seizure causes brief jerks of groups of muscles, often in the upper body. This kind of seizure often occurs just after a person wakes up.

▼ *If you see someone who has hurt themselves as a result of a seizure, you should call an ambulance and tell the medics exactly what you have seen.*

'When I fell over, my schoolfriends quickly moved all the desks and chairs away from me so I did not hurt myself. Afterwards I felt punch-drunk, like boxers must feel when they have been knocked out in the ring.'

Tom, aged 14, after a tonic-clonic seizure.

During an absence seizure, a person seems to be temporarily daydreaming or absent-minded. An absence seizure may last only a few seconds, but a person may experience hundreds in one day.

A tonic-clonic seizure is the most well-known generalised seizure. 'Tonic' is a medical term for when muscles stiffen, and 'clonic' describes when muscles contract and relax quickly in short bursts or spasms.

Stages of a tonic-clonic seizure

If you see someone having this type of generalised seizure, you may notice this in the tonic stage:

1 The person may make a loud cry or scream. This is not from pain or fear, but the result of air being squeezed out quickly from the lungs as chest muscles contract. He or she loses consciousness, stiffens and falls to the ground.

Then in the clonic stage:

2 Breathing may become noisy or the person may seem to stop breathing and may become pale or start to turn blue

3 The person's whole body starts to convulse (jerk or shake) rhythmically

4 The person may wet themselves as they have no control over their muscles

5 Finally, their muscles relax. The person usually regains consciousness at this time.

The after-effects

Following a tonic-clonic seizure, people can feel drowsy and may have a headache and want to sleep. This can last for some hours. Because their muscles have been overworked and stretched, they may feel aches and pains for some days after.

ANGELA'S STORY

Angela is 14 years old. When she was eight years old, she had meningitis, and soon after she experienced some tonic-clonic seizures. Then she was free from seizures for six years. Soon after her fourteenth birthday she experienced her first serious tonic-clonic seizure at home. Her mother describes what happened:

'Angela was sitting on a chair in the kitchen having breakfast. Out of the blue she said she felt a little strange. Then she made a strange sound, like a grunt, and fell off the chair onto the ground. Luckily she didn't hit anything, but she did knock her bowl of cereal off the table and it crashed to the ground. Angela's body stiffened briefly, then started jerking. She seemed to stop breathing for a few seconds. This lasted several minutes. I didn't panic because I knew she was having a seizure. I made sure she would not bash against anything, but I did not touch her. Gradually her muscles relaxed and she became conscious.'

Angela said afterwards: 'I really don't remember very much about the seizure. I felt tired for a long time afterwards.'

Triggers

Sometimes a situation or event sets off, or triggers, a seizure. It may be a flashing light, stress or tiredness. Once a person with epilepsy has established a trigger, he or she may be able to eliminate or reduce the number of seizures they have by avoiding situations that could bring on seizures. However, not everyone with epilepsy has a trigger.

Types of trigger

Several situations can trigger a seizure. Some people with epilepsy have seizures during times of stress, or when they are tired, bored or excited.

Light sensitivity

Changes in light can be a trigger. About 3-5 per cent of people with epilepsy are 'photosensitive' – they are affected by the flickering or flashing of lights at a disco or during a film, or the flickering of a computer screen. Watching television is not usually a problem unless it is in a dimly lit or unlit room. Taking a break from the screen every 30 minutes is a good idea. Some people with epilepsy find that wearing special, photochromic glasses can reduce the effect of these triggers.

▼ *For some people with epilepsy, looking at certain types of computer screen can trigger a seizure.*

▲ *Bright flashing lights, such as the stroboscopic (strobe) lights at a concert or rave, can trigger a seizure in people with certain types of epilepsy.*

Fatigue

Tiredness caused by too many late nights, jet lag or working night shifts can also act as a trigger for some people with epilepsy.

A healthy lifestyle

A healthy lifestyle is a good idea for everyone, not just people with epilepsy. Eating at least five portions of fruit and vegetables a day could help to fend off infections that make some people susceptible to a seizure.

Thresholds

Each person has a threshold for seizures. If the threshold is low, the person is more likely to experience seizures. The threshold may also be affected by such activities as drinking alcohol, taking recreational drugs or by hormonal imbalances in the body. All of these alter the activity of the brain and so make a person more susceptible to any trigger. For example, one person's threshold for a seizure may be exceeded after only one alcoholic drink, whereas another person may be able to have several drinks before they are affected.

Diagnosis

A person who has had a seizure should be seen by a doctor to check for the cause. As a routine, premature babies or babies whose birth was difficult will be examined by a hospital doctor to check for any brain condition. Similarly, people who have hurt their heads badly in an accident or suffered a serious brain infection, tumour or blood clot will be thoroughly examined to see if they are likely to develop seizures.

Building up a picture

Diagnosing epilepsy, identifying the causes and finding the best course of treatment are all carried out by a neurologist. A neurologist is a doctor specialising in the functioning and condition of the body's nervous system, including the brain. The neurologist will ideally examine a patient while he or she is having a seizure, but this is unlikely to be possible. Instead, they will ask family and friends to describe the frequency, symptoms and after-effects of the patient's seizures.

Different tests

Next, the neurologist may do a series of tests. First, he or she will try to find out if an illness could be the cause. This may involve doing a blood test to rule out other conditions, such as diabetes. Then the patient may have a test called an EEG, which records the pattern of electrical signals in the brain. Pads called electrodes are placed on the head, and these monitor how the brain reacts to possible triggers, such as flashing lights.

▶ *An MRI (Magnetic Resonance Imaging) scanner can be used to help diagnose epilepsy.*

Scans

The neurologist may perform a scan of the brain to look for any possible causes of the seizure using an MRI scanner. This uses the movement of water in the brain to build up an image, which is then displayed on a computer screen.

KHAN'S STORY

Khan is 10 years old and is susceptible to absence seizures.

'To prepare for my EEG, the neurologist, Dr Aziz, told me to have my breakfast early, at least two hours before my appointment at 10am. I was not to have any fizzy drinks or snacks after that, and I should take my anti-epileptic medicine as normal. I should wash my hair in baby shampoo so that my scalp was free from any oils or perfumes. When I got to his office, the nurse put some gel at various places on my scalp and attached about 20 electrodes. Then the EEG began.

On one occasion, Dr Aziz asked me to breathe rapidly and deeply for three minutes. This made me feel a little dizzy and tingly round the mouth. Then he asked me to close my eyes and he shone a flashing bright light in front of my eyes. The EEG lasted about an hour and did not hurt at all.

After my examination, Dr Aziz showed me my EEG scan on the computer screen. He showed me a scan of a normal 10-year old boy and compared it to mine. I could see that in places the lines on my scan had more ups and downs.'

▼ *An EEG measures the electrical activity of the brain by recording from electrodes, which are placed on the scalp.*

How you can help

The first time you see someone having a tonic-clonic seizure can be scary and unsettling. You cannot stop the seizure, but there are ways that you can help. The seizure will normally run its course in a few minutes. Staying calm will make you and any other onlookers feel more confident and reassured.

Dos and don'ts

1 Do stay close to the person and keep calm

2 Do move away any chairs, tables or other objects that the person could knock into

3 Do put something soft like a pillow or cushion under their head if they have fallen

4 Do not try to move the person

5 Do not put anything in the person's mouth

6 When the seizure is over, do try to roll the person onto his or her side in the 'recovery position' so that the airways are not blocked, and saliva can drain away

7 Do talk to the person, telling them what has happened. The person may feel embarrassed, so try to reassure them

8 If the person falls asleep afterwards, do regularly check if he or she is all right.

If the person having a seizure is someone you know and you are familiar with their symptoms, there is probably nothing more you need to do, other than check they do not hurt themselves during the seizure. If it is a stranger and you are not sure of their condition, check for a medi-alert tag (see page 28) once the seizure is over. If you are still unsure, call for an ambulance. However, some people have several seizures a month and they will be unsettled

▼ *Placing an unconscious person in the recovery position prevents their tongue from blocking their breathing and allows fluid to drain from their mouth. It is also a safe position to put someone in if you are forced to leave them alone.*

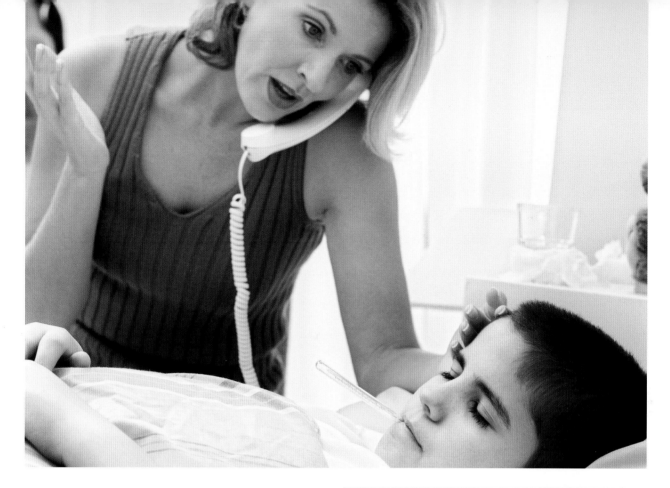

▲ *After a seizure the person affected may want to rest. If it is the first time a child has experienced a seizure, a parent or carer should consult a doctor, who may recommend tests and a brain scan.*

if they are taken to hospital every time. If people do hurt themselves during a seizure, give them first aid only if you are trained to do so. You can harm an injured person by moving them in the wrong way.

Emergency help

If you are unsure whether to call an ambulance, use the 'two and five minute' rule. If you know the person, and the seizure lasts two minutes longer than is normal, then call an ambulance. If you do not know the person, or you don't know how long their seizures usually last, call an ambulance if the seizure lasts for five minutes. Keep a record of when the seizure started and what happened. This will help the emergency services and doctors decide what treatment needs to be given.

TOM'S STORY

Tom experienced a tonic-clonic seizure when he was at a football match.

'My team had just scored and the next thing I remember was waking up near the touchline. The St. John Ambulance staff had brought me on a stretcher from the stands, where I had collapsed. Fortunately I was with my workmate, Derek, and he knew what to do. He waited till the seizure was over and then, just as a precaution, he called the ambulance. I was checked over and found to be fine. I stayed in the grounds till the match was over, then Derek took me home in a taxi. I slept all the way. At home I went straight to bed and felt fine in the morning.'

Controlling epilepsy

Because seizures can be upsetting, random and can lead to injury, it is important to try to reduce their frequency or prevent them. In about 70 per cent of people with epilepsy, drugs or medicines can do this. Avoiding the triggers that set off seizures will also help.

Drugs

Medicines used to prevent seizures are commonly known as anti-epileptic drugs (AEDs) or sometimes anti-convulsants. These work by reducing or eliminating the disruption of electrical signals in the brain, making the brain less susceptible to seizures. The medicines are taken regularly. As with any medicines, they can cause side effects, or unwanted reactions or feelings, such as skin rashes, sickness or tiredness. Patients may need to try several drugs until the best one is found.

STATUS EPILEPTICUS

There is a very serious type of situation called 'status epilepticus'. A person may have a continuous seizure lasting more than 30 minutes or a series of seizures without gaining consciousness in between. In extreme circumstances, and if not treated quickly with medication, the condition can cause death. In the United States, there are more than 100,000 incidents a year of status epilepticus and about 50,000 of them result in death.

Surgery

For those people who do not respond to drugs, surgery may be an option and may be necessary in cases where epilepsy is caused by brain damage or a tumour. Surgery usually involves removing the part

◀ *Anti-epileptic tablets. This drug, Epilim, reduces brain activity by increasing the amount of a chemical that blocks electrical messages passing from one neurone to another. During pregnancy, women may be advised to switch from Epilim.*

▲ Brain surgery is a way of curing some forms of epilepsy, but it is a delicate operation and carries risks.

of the brain responsible for the seizures. It is a very delicate operation as normal brain tissue must not be damaged — neurones cannot repair themselves.

RYAN'S STORY

Ryan had his first seizure when he was 32. An EEG helped show that his seizures were coming from a part of the left side of his brain. This had probably been caused 10 years earlier in a horse riding accident that left him unconscious for an hour. Over a period of five years, medication did not stop the seizures, so neurologists recommended carrying out surgery to remove the damaged part of his brain.

'The surgeon pointed out that there was only a 50 per cent chance that removal of the damaged part of my brain would solve the problem. He also made it clear how serious the operation would be: there was a possibility of damage to the speech and memory centres of my brain, and that recovery would take several months. Before the operation I had an EEG and an MRI scan and various tests to identify the exact location of the damaged part of my brain. During the operation I was occasionally woken to check no damage had been done to healthy tissues.'

After the operation, Ryan immediately became seizure-free, but after two years, the symptoms returned. He was put on new medication and has remained seizure-free for the last eight years.

Taking medicines

As soon as a person is diagnosed with epilepsy, doctors may prescribe drugs to get the condition under control. Because drugs can affect many different cells in the body, the doctor will be careful about what dosage to prescribe. If the original dose is not effective, the amount will be increased a little at a time until the right level is found. The drug is taken regularly to build up and maintain the level of the drug in the body.

Which medicine?

With more than 40 different types of seizure, there are many types of AEDs, or anti-convulsants, that can be used. The drugs may be taken by mouth as pills or tablets. They are usually taken two or three times a day, for example, one dose after breakfast in the morning and one after dinner in the evening. Very young children may take their medicines as syrups.

It is important to take the drugs at around the same time each day to maintain a constant level in the body. Some people store their drugs in a 'drug wallet'. This has see-through compartments for each day of the week to help remind them instantly whether or not they have taken the pills.

Like most medicines, AEDs can cause side effects in some people. For example, one type of AED has side effects that include tiredness, dizziness, blurred vision, skin rash and excitability. These can in turn affect concentration and thinking. Side effects of other anti-convulsants can include hair loss, weight gain and an abnormal heartbeat.

Complementary treatments

Some people do not like taking medicines. They may try to find more natural, or complementary, forms of treatment, including acupuncture, homeopathy and aromatherapy. None of these seem to be totally effective against epilepsy, but they may work alongside conventional medicines. Acupuncture involves using needles to stimulate the body's nervous system. Homeopathy tries to stimulate the body's own defence systems with natural substances. In aromatherapy, a person is exposed to the smell of various natural oils. All of these treatments should only be used under guidance from a neurologist and a complementary treatment specialist.

CARE WITH MEDICINES

Many pills and tablets look like little sweets, but if eaten by people who are not ill, or who have a condition other than epilepsy, they can be harmful. It is important medicines are kept safely away from small children.

ROBERT'S STORY

Robert is 12 years old.

'I have to take my anti-epileptic drugs three times a day, but I am a little forgetful. My parents have bought me a watch with alarms set for 8am, 2pm and 8pm to remind me to take my pills. During school terms, every Monday morning I give five pills to the head teacher, both for safekeeping and so that she can give me my afternoon pill each day. I keep my pills in a little box with a red cross and my name on it. At home my pillbox stays in my room. When I am out, I keep it in a little belt pouch and not in my pocket, where it may fall out. I have to make sure no other children can take my pills as they can harm someone who is not epileptic. My doctor and parents have told me that it is not serious if I miss a dose, and that everyone does this from time to time. However, this can cause some side effects so I should ask my teachers and friends to keep an eye on me when this happens.'

▼ *Some people try to ease the effects of epilepsy with acupuncture. It is thought that by stimulating the body's nervous system with needles, electrical disturbances in the brain can be controlled or overcome.*

Living with epilepsy

Most people with epilepsy lead normal lives if their seizures are controlled. If their medication works, they may never have another seizure. They can do most jobs and join in with most sports and leisure activities.

Carrying ID

To notify other people of their condition, many people with epilepsy wear a form of identification (ID), such as a medic-alert bracelet, wristband, tag or necklace. Sometimes these carry information about their seizures and medication. Other people carry an ID card with this information on.

Check-ups

People with epilepsy may visit their doctor or neurologist every few months to update their history of seizures and to check that their medicine is still working well. At each visit, the doctor will check that the medication and dose are still appropriate.

Should a person grow out of epilepsy or be seizure-free for more than two years, he or she may decide, together with the neurologist, to stop taking medication. However, each person is different and the risks and benefits of taking the medicine, or not taking it, have to be weighed up with the help of a neurologist. Taking any medicines when they are not needed is unnecessary and can be harmful.

Biofeedback

Some people with epilepsy are able to control their nervous activity to such a level that when they get an aura or unusual sensation, they can control their nerves so that a seizure does not happen. This is known as biofeedback. A person who uses biofeedback can control his or her body until it is able to regulate and correct itself naturally. To do this, a person with epilepsy has to learn how to interpret his or her EEG recordings and work out what to do to get any abnormal electrical activity in the brain under control. It requires a lot of testing, training and practice. Biofeedback is a difficult skill to develop and so it is not used very often.

◄ *Medical jewellery or ID tags contain important information about conditions such as epilepsy.*

Feeling confident and secure

Some people with epilepsy are worried about what will happen to them if they have a seizure. They are concerned how relatives, friends and people at school or work may react. They might wish to explain to everyone they know what type of epilepsy they have, what might happen, and what other people should do if they need help. However, not everyone with epilepsy will want to tell people about their condition.

HOW BIOFEEDBACK WORKS

In biofeedback – also known as neurofeedback – a person with epilepsy works with a computer to monitor their brain wave patterns. EEG scans are taken of a patient's brain activity and shown to the patient on a computer. Patients concentrate on relaxation techniques and on breathing in the hope of changing their brain activity.

Other training sessions use videos where, for example, a patient watching a video of a fish is asked to concentrate on changing it into other shapes, such as a mermaid and then a star. If the patient's emotional state changes, then the shapes on the video screen also change.

Because of the sophisticated technology that is used during biofeedback training sessions, this type of treatment can be very expensive and it is not available in all countries.

Epilepsy and families

For the parents, brothers and sisters of someone with epilepsy, small adjustments can be made to make life easier. For example, their house might be made very safe from minor accidents.

Safety at home

Just what safety features or practices would be helpful in the home depends on the type of seizure the person experiences and the things that trigger the seizure. Here are some examples:

1 Avoid furniture with sharp edges or cover the edges with foam or plastic

2 Avoid the person sleeping in a tall bunk bed in case he or she falls out during a seizure

3 Encourage the person not to lock the bathroom door or have a bath or shower without telling someone else in the house. An 'engaged' sign on the door can help

4 Have soft carpets on floors and stairs

5 Watch TV in a well-lit room

6 Fit safety glass to windows and doors

7 Use back burners or hotplates on a cooker and turn saucepan handles inwards so they cannot be knocked

8 Use electric kettles that switch off automatically.

▶ *Watching TV in a well-lit room can reduce the chances of a seizure for those people who are sensitive to flickering light.*

Epilepsy nurses

Some hospitals have special nurses who work with doctors and schools to give advice, information and help to people with epilepsy and their families. Epilepsy nurses may visit homes to advise on safety, dealing with a seizure and how to explain the condition to other people. They also give medical help and support to adults with epilepsy.

Family holidays

People with epilepsy sometimes talk to their doctor or neurologist before going on holiday to take advice on any activities that could trigger a seizure. Travelling by car, train or plane should not be a problem, but they should take food and drink for the journey to ensure they can have regular meals. They should also take enough medicine for their stay. With long-distance travel that crosses international time zones, the schedule for taking medicine may need to be adjusted to suit local times.

PET PATIENTS

Cats and dogs can have epilepsy. The causes, effects, symptoms and treatments of this condition in pets are very similar to human epilepsy. There are cases of pets experiencing a seizure on being taken to the vet, so it has been suggested that stress could be a cause.

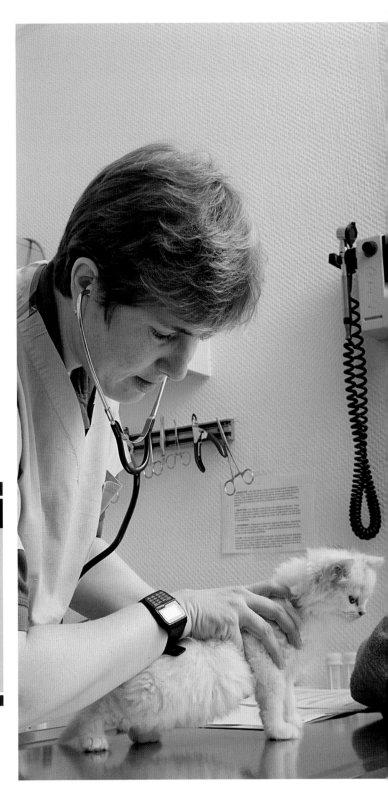

▶ *A pet with epilepsy requires similar attention and medication to a person with the condition. You should consult a vet if you think your pet may have had a seizure.*

Epilepsy at school

Most children with epilepsy attend mainstream schools and are able to join in all school activities. Teachers and pupils alike will benefit from learning about epilepsy and how to help a child who has the condition. However, not every school can provide the help and support needed, so some children will attend special learning centres.

Help is at hand

Any child of school age that develops epilepsy may have to take days off school until his or her medication is sorted out. The child may also find it difficult to concentrate in class and to do homework and exams. If they study for too long without a break, they can trigger a seizure. Epilepsy nurses may visit the school and help support the child when needed.

There are generally two main issues regarding epilepsy at school: the use of computers, and sports and outdoor activities. For those children likely to be affected by the flickering screens of computers, teachers should ensure the child works in a well-lit room and does not focus on the screen for too long at a time. For sports such as swimming, a child with epilepsy should be accompanied at all times in case help is needed.

School trips

Going on a school trip requires preparation and support. Children with epilepsy must take along their medication and remember to keep to the strict timetable for taking it. Parents, teachers and support staff can work together to ensure that the child can join in with all the activities.

Learning difficulties

Some children that have epilepsy as a result of brain damage at birth may find it difficult to learn at the same speed as other children. They may lack concentration or the ability to deal with lots of information and instructions and so may need special help with schoolwork. Many schools provide learning support teachers for this, and children work one-to-one with the teacher. Gradually, they may learn to read, write and do maths to high standards. Local epilepsy support groups often provide educational programmes to help parents and teachers set up schemes in schools.

Special schools

Children that regularly have seizures and often lose consciousness may wear a helmet to protect their head from injury should they fall down.

This can make them feel uneasy in a mainstream school. There are schools set up to help children with special needs. The children may live at the school during term time, and come home at weekends and in the holidays. At the school, teachers and helpers can make the children feel more confident.

▼ *Most children with epilepsy attend mainstream schools. Some children with epilepsy will not have any problem getting good grades, but others may need extra help.*

Sport and leisure

Sport is a healthy and enjoyable activity for everyone, including people with epilepsy. The benefits of regular exercise usually outweigh the risks from a possible seizure. Most sports are suitable for people with epilepsy, sometimes with just a few extra safety precautions.

Doctor's advice

It can be helpful for someone with epilepsy to discuss the possible dangers of an extreme sport with his or her neurologist or family doctor. Exercise is good for everyone and a person with epilepsy should keep active. However, he or she must take normal precautions, such as wearing a helmet for riding, cycling and other sports where a fall could result in a knock to the head.

Contact sports

Contact sports need to be considered carefully by a person with epilepsy. For example, boxing should be avoided, as a punch to the head could instantly cause a seizure. Rugby, too, can be dangerous for people who do not wear head protection, or for those with a low seizure threshold. People who have epilepsy sometimes try out a particular sport for a short time at first. Then, if they have no adverse reactions, they can gradually build up the time that they participate for.

▶ *Wearing a helmet when cycling is a sensible safety precaution for everyone. For people with epilepsy, who may have a seizure when cycling, it is essential.*

Gym activities

Using a treadmill and other gym equipment is generally fine for people with epilepsy. Some people with epilepsy have to be careful not to 'push themselves to the limit'. If they use a sauna or jacuzzi, they must ensure they do not get too hot as this can trigger a seizure.

Extreme sports

A person with epilepsy will have to consider carefully whether to take up extreme sports. Sports such as rock climbing may be dangerous for a person who

▼ *Usually, there is no reason why a person with epilepsy should not go to the gym to exercise, or go jogging.*

BOBBY JONES, OLYMPIC CHAMPION

Robert Clyde 'Bobby' Jones, born in 1951, is regarded as one of the best US basketball players of all time. He won a silver basketball team medal in the summer Olympic Games in Munich in 1972. He has had epilepsy since he was young.

experiences uncontrolled seizures. Scuba diving is something that is considered dangerous for people with epilepsy who have seizures or are taking anti-epileptic drugs.

Growing up with epilepsy

As a child's brain grows and fully develops, some forms of epilepsy may disappear.

Many people that have epilepsy as a child grow out of it in adulthood.

Adult life

In order to make sure that adults who have epilepsy keep safe, and to ensure the safety of those around them, governments have introduced various guidelines. Adults with epilepsy may not be allowed to hold certain jobs where health and safety could be at risk. For example, there are legal restrictions on the types of jobs that people with epilepsy can hold in the armed forces. In the UK, local councils decide whether a person with epilepsy can drive a taxi. If a person with epilepsy has been free of

▼ *Lewis Carroll was the pen name of Charles Lutwidge Dodgson (1832–1898), a mathematician, photographer and writer of children's books. His epilepsy influenced his work.*

IN WONDERLAND: THE STORY OF LEWIS CARROLL

As an adult, English author Lewis Carroll developed epilepsy and had severe headaches and migraines. Carroll recorded his seizures, and how they affected his writing, in his journals. In his diaries he used such terms and expressions as 'fits', 'eerie states' and 'the waking dream'. In his famous books, *Alice in Wonderland* and *Alice Through the Looking Glass*, Alice finds herself growing and shrinking, seeing objects larger and smaller than reality, and falling down holes. It may be that these were Carroll's way of describing his seizures.

seizures for a year, he or she is allowed to drive a car. If a person only has seizures during their sleep for three years, he or she will also be allowed to drive a car.

Fighting discrimination

The Disability Discrimination Act ensures that a person who has a disability, such as epilepsy, must have the same conditions of employment as someone without the condition. Even someone who has had epilepsy in the past, but is no longer affected by it, is covered by the Act. An employer cannot use epilepsy as an excuse for not promoting someone, not giving them a pay rise or not paying sickness benefits.

▼ *People with epilepsy might use a panic alarm like this to get help if they hurt themselves during a seizure.*

Brain damage

For a person that develops epilepsy as an adult, some adjustment to everyday life may need to be made. There is generally less support for adults than for children with the condition, and the side effects of medication may influence their lives differently. Often, epilepsy in adulthood develops as a result of a stroke or brain damage caused in an accident, but there are lots of possible causes.

In later life

Some people of retirement age naturally experience loss of memory, and those with epilepsy may find this gets worse as a side effect of their anti-epileptic drugs. This in turn may make them more likely to forget to take their medication regularly, which can make them more dependent on their alarms and helpers.

The future for epilepsy

There is constant research going on to try to treat epilepsy, but neurologists are not yet close to preventing or curing epilepsy completely. However, brain surgery is now possible without opening a person's skull, and anti-epileptic drugs are becoming more effective, with fewer side effects.

Laser surgery and implants

Using the intense energy of a laser beam, surgeons can now cut away damaged parts of the brain or brain tumours without making major incisions. The beam can be accurately directed at a tiny part of the brain so that there is little danger of damage to healthy tissues. This laser surgery can be used to cure some types of epilepsy.

Vagus nerve stimulation

One technique used to treat epilepsy is vagus nerve stimulation. This involves implanting a small electrical device under the skin below the left collar bone. Wires from the device are wrapped around the person's vagus nerve in the neck in a small operation. The vagus nerve carries messages to and from major control centres in the brain. A neurologist can program the device to send impulses that try to prevent seizures. If a person senses a seizure coming on, they can activate the device to send extra messages to the brain to prevent it.

Robotic devices

One day, it may be possible to implant devices that automatically sense when a seizure is about to happen. Scientists have already developed some miniature computerised 'robotic' devices that, once inserted in the bloodstream, can detect the levels of various chemicals in the body. If such devices could sense the sudden, irregular surges of nerve impulses that trigger a seizure and send out counter-signals, a complete cure for epilepsy may be possible.

SEIZURE DOGS

There are dogs that can sense their owner's seizure about 30 seconds before it happens. It is not exactly understood how the dogs do this. It could be that they notice their owner behaving differently or sense an unusual body odour, electrical signals or other aura. The dogs are trained to bark or press against the person or to sit down and not move to warn that a seizure is about to happen.

▶ *This six-year-old girl has inherited a form of epilepsy that randomly produces rapid jerks of her body lasting less than a second. Rooney, her dog, is a seizure dog, trained to alert her when she is about to have an attack.*

Glossary

absence seizure a seizure in which the person appears to be vacant or daydreaming for a few moments. Used to be called a petit mal

acupuncture a technique developed in Chinese medicine that treats ailments and other problems by inserting special needles into specific places in the body

anti-epileptic drug (AED) a medicine or drug used to control the symptoms of epilepsy. Also known as an anti-convulsant

aura a partial seizure that acts as a warning of a generalised seizure

complementary treatment treatment that helps, or works alongside, the main treatment. Often it is not known how effective a complementary medicine actually is

contract to become smaller or narrower

diabetes a condition where the body does not produce enough insulin, a hormone that breaks down sugar in the blood

diagnose to identify a condition or disease after careful examination of the body and symptoms

DNA short for Deoxyribonucleic acid, a molecule that contains the genetic instructions for how a living being lives and grows

EEG a recording device known as an electroencephalogram. It records electrical activity in the brain

epilepsy a condition of the brain involving irregular electrical activity that can result in seizures

generalised seizure a seizure that affects the whole brain from its onset and causes a person to lose consciousness

grand mal a term once used for a tonic-clonic seizure

hormonal to do with hormones, substances produced by the body that regulate how various organs work

incision a small cut used in surgery

MRI a scanner known as a magnetic resonance imaging device

nerves cells in the body that make up the nervous system, including the brain. Groups of neurones (brain cells) make up nerves

nervous system the network made up of nerves, the spinal column and the brain

neurologist a doctor who specialises in the health, conditions, diseases and treatment of the brain

neurones scientific name for nerve cells. These communicate with one another and other parts of the body via electrical signals

partial seizure a type of seizure that affects only a part of the brain

petit mal a term once used for absence seizures

photochromic a clear glass that can darken when exposed to bright light

saliva a liquid made in the mouth

seizure any type of irregular electrical activity in the brain. An epileptic seizure causes a person to feel strange, uneasy and maybe fall to the ground unconscious and twitch or jerk. It can last from a few seconds to several minutes

siblings brothers and sisters

side effects unwanted symptoms of any medical treatment including the taking of medicines

stroke the bursting of a blood vessel in the brain

symptoms changes in the body that can indicate that a disease or other condition is present

synapses narrow gaps in between neurones, across which neurones pass messages to each other using electrical signals

tonic-clonic seizure a severe type of seizure where a person loses consciousness and experiences convulsions

trigger something that sets something else off; for example, flashing lights can trigger an epileptic seizure

tumour an abnormal mass of cells

vagus nerve a group of nerve fibres that carry signals to and from the brain, down through the neck, to the digestive system and heart. Many of the signals are related to the body's automatic actions

Further information

Books

Fiction

Total Football: Injury Time,
Alan Gibbons, *Orion Childrens, 2010*

Non-Fiction

Epilepsy - The Ultimate Teen Guide,
Kathlyn Gay and Sean McGarrahan,
Scarecrow Press, 2002/2007

Coping with Epilepsy,
Fiona Marshall and Dr Pamela Crawford,
Sheldon Press, 2006

My Friend has Epilepsy, Anna Levene,
Chrysalis Children's Books, 2003

Websites

www.epilepsy.org.uk
The Epilepsy Action website offers advice, the number of a helpline and runs campaigns, conferences and a forum. Check out 'you got nerves', the section of the website for teenagers affected by epilepsy.

www.epilepsynse.org.uk
The National Society for Epilepsy (NSE) is the largest epilepsy charity in the UK. NSE produces a range of information resources including leaflets, factsheets and DVDs on a range of issues around epilepsy. Their national confidential helpline is available to anyone wanting information or support. NSE's website includes information about epilepsy and an epilepsy forum where you can chat to other people with epilepsy.

www.ncype.org.uk
The National Centre for Young People with Epilepsy provides education, rehabilitation, treatment and care for children and young people between the ages of five and 25 who have epilepsy.

www.epilepsyresearch.org.uk
Epilepsy Research UK – From this website you can download leaflets on what causes epilepsy, the types of epilepsy and tips on epilepsy first aid.

www.aesnet.org
The American Epilepsy Society promotes research and education for doctors and health workers who treat people with epilepsy.

www.epilepsyfoundation.org
This website offers specific advice and information on how epilepsy affects different age groups, from children, to teens, to parents and the elderly. Also has a useful page on first aid tips.

www.epilepsy.org.au
The Epilepsy Action Australia website has information about epilepsy, a glossary of medical terms and useful first aid information, as well as tips on making homes and workplaces safe for people who are prone to seizures.

Note to parents and teachers: Every effort has been made by the Publishers to ensure that these websites are suitable for children, that they are of the highest educational value, and that they contain no inappropriate or offensive material. However, because of the nature of the Internet, it is impossible to guarantee that the contents of these sites will not be altered. We strongly advise that Internet access is supervised by a responsible adult.

Index

These are the list of contents for each title in Explaining:

Asthma

What is asthma? • History of asthma • Increase in asthma • Who has asthma? • Healthy lungs • How asthma affects the lungs • What triggers asthma? • Asthma and allergies • Diagnosing asthma • Preventing an attack • Relieving an attack • What to do during an attack • Growing up with asthma • Living with asthma • Asthma and exercise • Future

Autism

What is autism? • Autism: a brief history • The rise of autism • The autistic spectrum • The signs of autism • Autism and inheritance • The triggers of autism • Autism and the body • Autism and mental health • Can autism be treated? • Living with autism • Autism and families • Autism and school • Asperger syndrome • Autism and adulthood • The future for autism

Blindness

What is blindness? • Causes and effects • Visual impairment • Colour blindness and night blindness • Eye tests • Treatments and cures • Coping with blindness • Optical aids • Guide dogs and canes • Home life • On the move • Blindness and families • Blindness at school • Blindness as an adult • Blindness, sport and leisure • The future for blindness

Cerebral Palsy

What is cerebral palsy? • The causes of cerebral palsy • Diagnosis • Types of cerebral palsy • Other effects of cerebral palsy • Managing cerebral palsy • Other support • Technological support • Communication • How it feels • Everyday life • Being at school • Cerebral palsy and the family • Into adulthood • Raising awareness • The future

Cystic Fibrosis

What is cystic fibrosis? • A brief history • What causes cystic fibrosis? • Screening and diagnosis • The effects of cystic fibrosis • How is cystic fibrosis managed? • Infections and illness • A special diet • Clearing the airways • Physical exercise • Cystic fibrosis and families • Cystic fibrosis at school • Living with cystic fibrosis • Living longer • New treatments • Gene therapy

Deafness

What is deafness? • Ears and sounds • Types of deafness • Causes of deafness • Signs of deafness • Diagnosis • Treating deafness • Lip reading • Sign language • Deafness and education • Schools for the deaf • Deafness and adulthood • Technology • Deafness and the family • Fighting discrimination • Latest research

Diabetes

What is diabetes? • Type 1 diabetes • Type 2 diabetes • Symptoms and diagnosis • Medication • Hypoglycaemia • Eyes, skin and feet • Other health issues • Healthy eating and drinking • Physical activity • Living with diabetes • Diabetes and families • Diabetes at school • Growing up with diabetes • The future for diabetics

Down's syndrome

What is Down's syndrome? • Changing attitudes • Who has Down's Syndrome? • What are chromosomes? • The extra chromosome • Individual differences • Health problems • Testing for Down's Syndrome • Diagnosing at birth • Babies • Toddlers • At school • Friendships and fun • Effects on the family • Living independently • Down's syndrome community

Epilepsy

What is epilepsy? • Causes and effects • Who has epilepsy? • Partial seizures • Generalised seizures • Triggers • Diagnosis • How you can help • Controlling epilepsy • Taking medicines • Living with epilepsy • Epilepsy and families • Epilepsy at school • Sport and leisure • Growing up with epilepsy • The future for epilepsy

Food allergy

What are food allergies? • Food allergies: a brief history • Food aversion, intolerance or allergy? • What is an allergic reaction? • Food allergies: common culprits • Anaphylaxis • Testing for food allergies • Avoiding allergic reactions • Treating allergic reactions • Food allergies on the rise • Food allergies and families • Food allergies and age • Living with food allergies • 21st century problems • The future for food allergies